Tattooed You

ADULT COLORING BOOK

Tattoos are the stories in your heart, written on your skin.
Charles De Lint, The Mystery of Grace

⚘ SEARCH & COLOR ⚘

A UNIQUE AND INTRICATE COLORING BOOK DESIGNED FOR ADULTS
38 DESIGNS TO BRING OUT THE BEST IN YOUR CREATIVENESS PROWESS

PLEASE NOTE: This is <u>not</u> a children's coloring book.
Images are intricately detailed and will require 100% of your attention.

ENJOY!

All rights reserved. No part of this book may be reproduced in any form, or by any electronic means, including information storage and retrieval systems, without permission in writing from the publisher.

Copyright © 2017 Dawné Dominique
ISBN: 978-1-7750442-3-9
Cover and Art Designed by Dawné Dominique
Vector Copyrights © VectorStock & DepositPhotos

Published by DusktilDawn Publications
www.dusktildawndesigns.com
CANADA

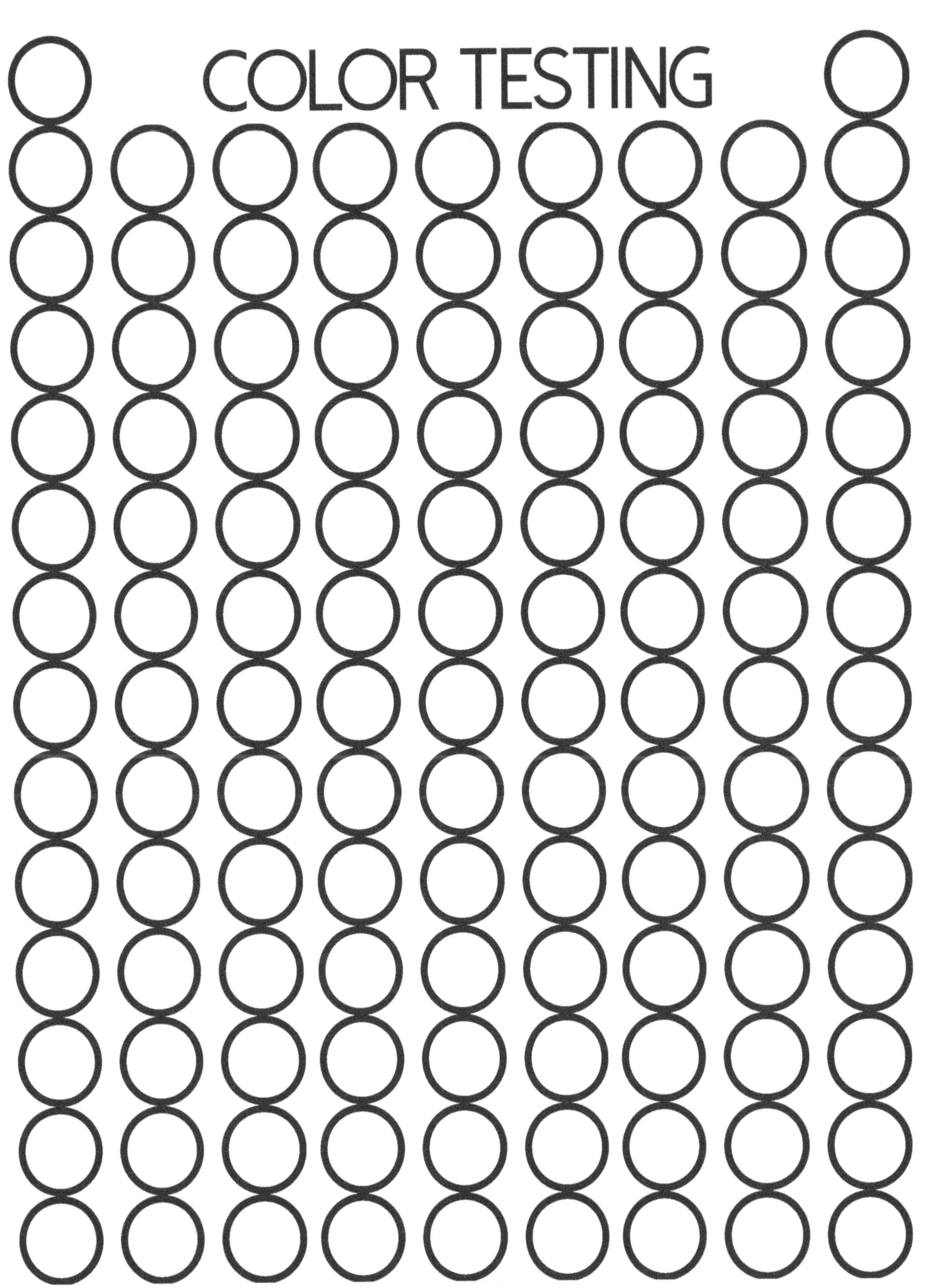

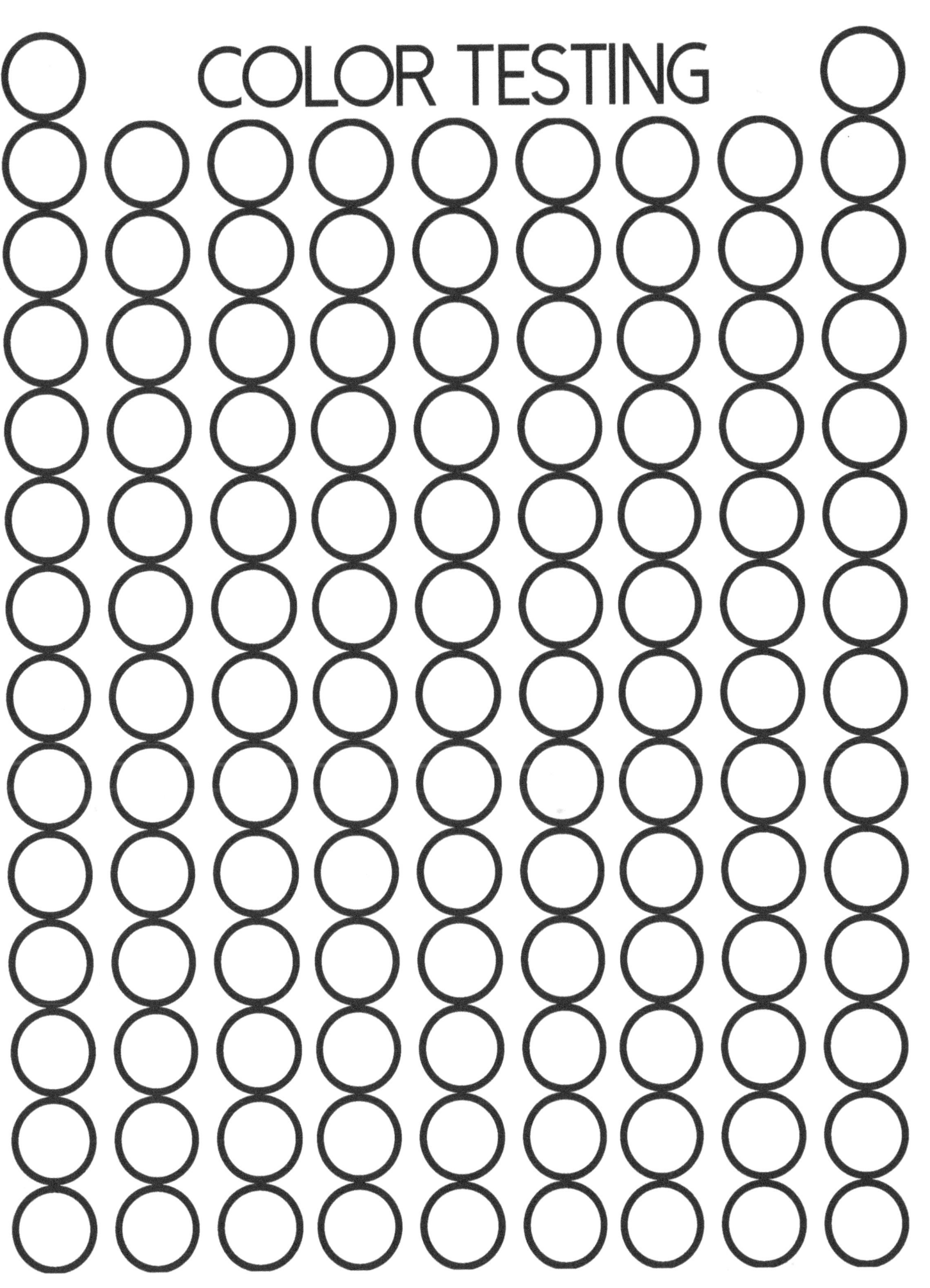

IF YOU ENJOYED THIS COLORING BOOK, DON'T BE SHY...LEAVE A REVIEW.

Check out other adult coloring books by Dawné Dominique & D. Thomas-Jerlo

www.lulu.com/spotlight/dusktildawn

Also available at:

www.dusktildawndesigns.com

www.ingramcontent.com/pod-product-compliance
Lightning Source LLC
Chambersburg PA
CBHW080448110426
42743CB00016B/3317